GW00401748

Miche... Leggott

BORN
TO
SHOP

SUMMERSDALE

Summersdale Publishers Ltd
46 West Street
Chichester
PO19 1RP

www.summersdale.com

ISBN 1 84024 198 5

Printed and bound in Great Britain

Text by Michelle Leggatt
Cartoons by Kate Taylor

You know you're a shopaholic when . . .

You buy the same pair of shoes in three colours because they're 'comfy'.

4

You distract your best
friend so that she doesn't
spot the sexy black dress
before you do.

You think of your pay rise
in terms of new outfits
rather than pounds
and pence.

YOU KNOW YOU'RE A SHOPAHOLIC WHEN . . .

Your ideal holiday is a shopping trip to New York.

YOU KNOW YOU'RE A SHOPAHOLIC WHEN . . .

You take a sickie and indulge in a spot of retail therapy.

YOU KNOW YOU'RE A SHOPAHOLIC WHEN . . .

Window shopping is more satisfying than sex.

YOU KNOW YOU'RE A SHOPAHOLIC WHEN . . .

Even a trip to your local supermarket is seen as an adventure.

YOU KNOW YOU'RE A SHOPAHOLIC WHEN . . .

You spend an extra £50 to get 5 more points on your reward card.

YOU KNOW YOU'RE A SHOPAHOLIC WHEN . . .

Your store card collection is bigger than your CD collection.

YOU KNOW YOU'RE A SHOPAHOLIC WHEN . . .

Your annual shopping bill in
Harvey Nicks exceeds the
GNP of Latin America.

Even a Tupperware party is
seen as a not-to-be-missed
shopping spree.

Your till receipts are
longer than toilet rolls.

18

YOU KNOW YOU'RE A SHOPAHOLIC WHEN . . .

Wearing the right outfit to
complement the latest
swanky boutique bag
is a must.

You wheel a pushchair round the high street with no baby in it. Well, carrying all those bags is hard work!

YOU KNOW YOU'RE A SHOPAHOLIC WHEN . . .

You are the millionth customer in more than one store.

YOU KNOW YOU'RE A SHOPAHOLIC WHEN . . .

You have a wardrobe full of clothes but nothing to wear to the office party.

You pay more attention to
the adverts than the actual
programmes on the telly.

YOU KNOW YOU'RE A SHOPAHOLIC WHEN . . .

sssh......the adverts are on.....

YOU KNOW YOU'RE A SHOPAHOLIC WHEN . . .

The manager at your local
department store knows
you by your first name.

YOU KNOW YOU'RE A SHOPAHOLIC WHEN . . .

Every purchase is made on
a different credit card.

You know more about the merchandise in your fave boutique than the sales assistants.

You never take your
boyfriend shopping with
you – he'd only slow
you down.

YOU KNOW YOU'RE A SHOPAHOLIC WHEN . . .

Shopping assistants turn
up at your wedding.

YOU KNOW YOU'RE A SHOPAHOLIC WHEN . . .

Security guards greet you like a long lost friend.

YOU KNOW YOU'RE A SHOPAHOLIC WHEN . . .

You walk the dog the long way round to gaze at the leather trousers you're going to buy at the weekend.

YOU KNOW YOU'RE A SHOPAHOLIC WHEN . . .

You fantasise about presenting QVC.

You're knocked over by a
bus and outfits not bought
– rather than snapshots of
your life – flash before
your eyes.

You collect store cards
like your kids collect
Pokemon cards.

36

YOU KNOW YOU'RE A SHOPAHOLIC WHEN . . .

You know the exact dates of the summer sales three years in advance.

You convince yourself you'll
have slimmed down from a
size 14 to an 8 to fit into
that Conran dress in time
for the office party – well,
it was such a bargain!

YOU KNOW YOU'RE A SHOPAHOLIC WHEN . . .

YOU KNOW YOU'RE A SHOPAHOLIC WHEN . . .

Your shopping trolley needs an HGV licence.

You can't wait 'til Christmas is over to attack the sales...they're far more fun than mince pies and family gatherings!

YOU KNOW YOU'RE A SHOPAHOLIC WHEN . . .

When the salesgirl says you look good in an outfit you genuinely believe her even though she's busy filing her nails.

YOU KNOW YOU'RE A SHOPAHOLIC WHEN . . .

You're the subject of a TV
documentary for obsessive
compulsive disorder.

44

YOU KNOW YOU'RE A SHOPAHOLIC WHEN . . .

Everyone you know asks *you* for the latest fashion advice rather than waiting to read it in a magazine.

YOU KNOW YOU'RE A SHOPAHOLIC WHEN . . .

Your monthly bank statement reads like a *Who's Who* of high street chic.

You spend so long at your local shopping centre your car parking bill is more than your shopping!

47

YOU KNOW YOU'RE A SHOPAHOLIC WHEN . . .

You are featured on a missing persons appeal after a particularly lengthy shopping spree.

YOU KNOW YOU'RE A SHOPAHOLIC WHEN . . .

You are asked to be the guest speaker at the monthly WI meeting to talk about 'The Perils of Living Beyond Your Means'.

YOU KNOW YOU'RE A SHOPAHOLIC WHEN . . .

You go into town and exchange 80% of the presents you got for your birthday as an excuse for another shopping trip.

You programme the sound
of a cash register into your
mobile as its ringing tone.

52

YOU KNOW YOU'RE A SHOPAHOLIC WHEN . . .

You buy CDs of your favourite in-store muzak to remind you of happy hours spent shopping.

YOU KNOW YOU'RE A SHOPAHOLIC WHEN . . .

You meet and fall in love
with your future husband
at the customer service
counter of M&S.

YOU KNOW YOU'RE A SHOPAHOLIC WHEN . . .

You have to build an
extension to house
all your outfits.

YOU KNOW YOU'RE A SHOPAHOLIC WHEN . . .

You christen your daughter
Emma *Dorothy*
Perkins Smith.

You realise you're a nightmare to buy presents for as you've already got everything.

YOU KNOW YOU'RE A SHOPAHOLIC WHEN . . .

Your little brother does a
school project on you.

YOU KNOW YOU'RE A SHOPAHOLIC WHEN . . .

You attend a school reunion and are shocked that they haven't changed the curtains in the hall since you left.

On a date, the only way you can reach orgasm is by thinking about the guy's bank balance.

YOU KNOW YOU'RE A SHOPAHOLIC WHEN . . .

You buy a bigger car even though you've got no kids...well, the bags have got to go somewhere!

You take up self-defence
classes to prepare yourself
for the New Year sales.

YOU KNOW YOU'RE A SHOPAHOLIC WHEN . . .

You exchange Christmas cards with the centre manager of your local shopping centre.

Your recurring nightmare
is that your car won't start
on the morning
of the sales.

You frame your Harvey
Nicks and Harrods
till receipts.

Your husband names
Harvey Nicks as the reason
for your divorce.

You can find your way
round town
blindfolded...literally!

You dress your boyfriend
to co-ordinate with
your outfits.

YOU KNOW YOU'RE A SHOPAHOLIC WHEN . . .

Your husband suggests
that he registers himself
as a charity.

YOU KNOW YOU'RE A SHOPAHOLIC WHEN . . .

You check into the hotel nearest the local shopping centre on the first night of your honeymoon.

YOU KNOW YOU'RE A SHOPAHOLIC WHEN . . .

You move house to be
nearer to the
High Street.

YOU KNOW YOU'RE A SHOPAHOLIC WHEN . . .

You can't remember your first kiss but joyfully recall your first sale bargain.

YOU KNOW YOU'RE A SHOPAHOLIC WHEN . . .

You go part time at work to be able to spend more time shopping.

YOU KNOW YOU'RE A SHOPAHOLIC WHEN . . .

You telephone ahead and bribe the sales assistant to put the last size 12 dress aside for you when you find out your friend is headed that way.

You are sectioned for your
shopping addiction, but still
manage to spend money in
the hospital shop

YOU KNOW YOU'RE A SHOPAHOLIC WHEN . . .

You know all the codes for
your favourite catalogue
items off by heart.

You can recognise goods
just by their bar codes.

You volunteer to organise
your office annual outing
and take your colleagues
to Bluewater.

YOU KNOW YOU'RE A SHOPAHOLIC WHEN . . .

Your average shopping trip takes longer than most people's annual holiday.

You lobby government regularly to abolish early Sunday closing.

YOU KNOW YOU'RE A SHOPAHOLIC WHEN . . .

YOU KNOW YOU'RE A SHOPAHOLIC WHEN . . .

Your idea of heaven is
having a personal shopper
rather than a
personal stereo.

YOU KNOW YOU'RE A SHOPAHOLIC WHEN . . .

You always carry a notepad,
tape measure and
calculator in your bag...
just in case!

You hate stripping off for the doctor but have no qualms in the communal changing room of your favourite boutique.

YOU KNOW YOU'RE A SHOPAHOLIC WHEN . . .

You firmly believe that the person who invented 'buy one get one free' should be made a saint.

YOU KNOW YOU'RE A SHOPAHOLIC WHEN . . .

Your blood pressure increases at the sight of a Prada handbag.

YOU KNOW YOU'RE A SHOPAHOLIC WHEN . . .

You only date guys with
Armani charge cards.

YOU KNOW YOU'RE A SHOPAHOLIC WHEN . . .

An ideal first date is being taken to London and being let loose on Oxford Street with his credit card.

You think nothing of getting up at 4am to be first in line at the New Year sales.

You log on to the internet home shopping sites more often than those that might actually help you finish your essay.

You find that even a trip round the garden centre with the kids dispels those Sunday blues.

You acknowledge that some
days window shopping is
just not enough.

You convince yourself that
accompanying your husband
to the DIY store is more
fun than just staying in.

YOU KNOW YOU'RE A SHOPAHOLIC WHEN . . .

You barricade yourself into
your house to avoid any
disastrous shopping
mistakes during that time
of the month.

You only ever ask for gift
vouchers as presents – why
should anyone else choose
what you want?

Mental arithmetic is your
strongest subject...all
those shopping problems –
it's second nature!

You buy two of everything
– just in case you break
the first one.

You throw an obscene
amount of parties so that
you always have the
perfect excuse to shop for
a new outfit.

YOU KNOW YOU'RE A SHOPAHOLIC WHEN . . .

You raid your son's piggy bank to get your daily fix.

You get a pet dog to give
you with the perfect
excuse to buy expensive –
but essential – accessories.

YOU KNOW YOU'RE A SHOPAHOLIC WHEN . . .

YOU KNOW YOU'RE A SHOPAHOLIC WHEN . . .

You plan your business meetings around towns with good shopping facilities.

YOU KNOW YOU'RE A SHOPAHOLIC WHEN . . .

You don't believe in
insurance or guarantees –
if it breaks, get a new one.

YOU KNOW YOU'RE A SHOPAHOLIC WHEN . . .

You actually want your husband to ask you to host a business dinner so that you can go wild in the supermarket even if his boss is an all-time bore.

You never buy a new
lipstick without getting the
matching nail varnish
as well.

YOU KNOW YOU'RE A SHOPAHOLIC WHEN . . .

You take up a new hobby every other month just so that you can buy a whole new set of essential equipment.

YOU KNOW YOU'RE A SHOPAHOLIC WHEN . . .

You believe that the more store cards you have the greater your status in your girlfriends' eyes.

Credit card companies
invite you to their annual
gala dinner for privileged
customers.

You treat a blue cross day
like *Mission Impossible*.

YOU KNOW YOU'RE A SHOPAHOLIC WHEN . . .

You size up people by their time spent shopping.

The bus driver doesn't ask
for your destination and
just says, "Your usual?"

YOU KNOW YOU'RE A SHOPAHOLIC WHEN . . .

You continuously hum store jingles.

YOU KNOW YOU'RE A SHOPAHOLIC WHEN . . .

You almost crash the car straining to take in a new window display.

YOU KNOW YOU'RE A SHOPAHOLIC WHEN . . .

YOU KNOW YOU'RE A SHOPAHOLIC WHEN . . .

You treat yourself to 'something special' more than once a week.

YOU KNOW YOU'RE A SHOPAHOLIC WHEN . . .

YOU KNOW YOU'RE A SHOPAHOLIC WHEN . . .

You always carry a spare bag with you 'just in case'...

YOU KNOW YOU'RE A SHOPAHOLIC WHEN . . .

You happily volunteer to take grannie shopping every week.

You get a thrill of pleasure
from signing a Visa slip.

You forget to collect your
dry cleaning on purpose so
that you'll have an excuse
to replace that 'tired old'
work suit.

Even on Safari, there's just
no stopping you.

YOU KNOW YOU'RE A SHOPAHOLIC WHEN . . .

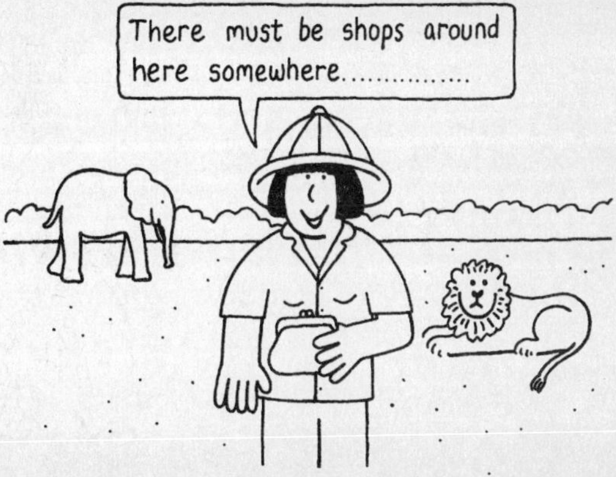

**For the latest humour books
from Summersdale, check out**

www.summersdale.com